Bunnies A-Z

Bunny Care & Behavior

Tracy Meadows

Bunnies A-Z © 2018 by Tracy Meadows

All rights reserved. No part of this book may be used, reproduced or transmitted in any form or by any means, electronic, mechanical, or otherwise, including photocopying, recording, or by any information storage or retrieval system, without written permission from the publisher, except in the case of brief quotations embodied in critical articles and reviews.

The Bossy Bunny first edition 2018

Cover photo by Cat Angels Photography

Logo by Sean Cochran

www.TheBossyBunny.com

PO Box 90023

Raleigh, NC 27675

Tracy@TheBossyBunny.com

Published in the United States of America by The Bossy Bunny

Copyright © 2018 Tracy Meadows

All rights reserved

ISBN: 0692070931

ISBN-13: 978-0692070932

Dedication

This book is dedicated to my amazing nephew, Brandon. You make us all proud. Thank you for your service to our country. We love you.

Bunnies A-Z

CONTENTS

	Acknowledgements	i
A	Attitude	Pg. 1-2
B	Bathing	Pg. 3-4
C	Chewing	Pg. 5-6
D	Destructive	Pg. 7-8
E	Ears	Pg. 9-10
F	Friends	Pg. 11-12
G	Grooming	Pg. 13-14
H	Herbs	Pg. 15-16
I	Intelligent	Pg. 17-18
J	Jumping	Pg. 19-20
K	Kisses	Pg. 21-22
L	Litter box	Pg. 23-24
M	Messy	Pg. 25-26
N	Noises	Pg. 27-28
O	Occupy	Pg. 29-30
P	Poop	Pg. 31-32
Q	Quirky	Pg. 33-34

R	Research	Pg. 35-36
S	Snacks	Pg. 37-38
T	Tunnels	Pg. 39-40
U	Unlimited Hay & Water	Pg. 41-42
V	Vegetables	Pg. 43-44
W	Wild Rabbits	Pg. 45-46
X	X-Pen (exercise pen)	Pg. 47-48
Y	Yawn	Pg. 49-50
Z	Zonked	Pg. 51-52

Appendix	Pg. 53
Vegetables Continued	Pg. 54
Natasha's Rescue	Pg. 55-56
Health & Wellness Tips	Pg. 57-58
The Life of an Easter Bunny review	Pg. 59
Special Thanks and Photo Credits	Pg. 60-61

Acknowledgements

There are so many people thank, but I especially want to highlight a few here.

So many friends have listened to me talk about this crazy idea I had about creating an ABC picture book on bunny care and behavior. Thank you for not telling me to stop talking and take a hike. Look! The book is real!

Michelle Zeman, I appreciate you so much. You have been so supportive with my first book. You've shared it at events when you were there to sell your own books, Chronicles of a Wererabbit (which is my favorite series, by the way). You have been just as supportive with this book. When your series hits Harry Potter and Hunger Games status, I will be able to say, "I knew her before she was famous."

Linda Culbert, you have given me such peace of mind by proofreading and editing this book. Your love and knowledge for proper grammar and for bunnies made you a perfect choice. Thank you from the bottom of my heart. Thank you for sharing Ezra and Duck pictures with me, too.

Full Disclaimer: Errors on this page should not be held against Linda. She did not see this page.

Liz Incardone, from the beginning, you have always been there with your insane bunny knowledge. To be clear, I'm not saying you are insane, just the amount of bunny knowledge you have in your brain is insane. Thank you for being a great mentor and a wonderful friend.

Thank you to my partner in crime, my husband, Greg. You jumped on board this crazy bunny train with me and have been supportive from the beginning. You even got genuinely excited the first moment I mentioned the crazy thought I had about writing a bunny book. Your support means everything to me. Love you most.

I will always be thankful to our little Suzie. Because of her, I have met some amazing friends online and in person. She is always a hit with her fans. She keeps it real.

This is one of Suzie's Glamour Shots from MidWest Bunfest 2016.

See page 59 for more acknowledgements to the wonderful photo contributors.

In memory of all the amazing bunnies we have lost.

Attitude

Bunnies are soft, cute, quiet, cuddly, and full of attitude. Mess with their stuff and you will see the attitude. You'll likely see it when you try to clean out their area, including their litter box. It is best to clean their space when they are running around and not paying attention to you. Every bunny shows it in a different way. Some bunnies will nip at you, thump their foot, grunt, or just stare. This stare is known in the bunny groups as a "disapproving bunny." If you share your home with a bunny, you are guaranteed to witness such attitude at some point. They have no idea how cute they are when they try to look and act ferocious.

Pumpkin, Queen of Attitude in her home. Not being petted before the other bunnies, meals not being served on time, when her paws have to touch linoleum because the fleece is not perfectly placed on the floor, are all things that give this cutie an attitude! Photo courtesy of Justina Hoflock

When Kepler was told not to chew his mom's pants, he let her know, in no uncertain terms, that he was not impressed with her response to his project. Guess he will have to find a new project.

Photo courtesy of Luci Finucan

When Yorgi is denied more treats, she demands a recount, she will stare in disapproval until the recount is complete and the results lean in her favor. Human treat limit and bunny treat limit do not equal the same number.

Photo courtesy of Michelle Zeman, author of the Chronicles of a Wererabbit

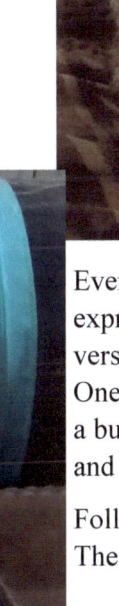

Every bunny has their own way of expressing attitude, but the one universal sign seems to be "the butt!" One has not been truly snubbed by a bunny until one has been ignored and shown the bunny butt.

Follow Suzie's ongoing saga on The Bossy Bunny Facebook page.

Bathing

You should never put your bunny in water. Bunnies are very fragile animals and submerging them in water can cause them to go into shock and possibly die.

When bunnies have been kept in undesirable living conditions, they may develop urine stains on their feet. Those stains will generally wear off in time without subjecting them to water, assuming their living conditions have changed.

There are times when a bunny may need to be "freshened" up for one reason or another. I have personally used the dry method on Suzie and it worked very well.

It's always best to check with your bunny savvy veterinarian to find out the cause of your bunny's soiled bottom.

Occasionally bunnies will get a "poopy butt" for whatever reason and a "butt bath" may be needed. You may want to try one of the following methods to get bunny's butt clean.

Wet Butt Bath Method

1. Line a small litter box with a towel for traction.
2. Fill box with 1-2 inches of warm water. Soap/shampoo is not needed.
3. Hold front of bunny upright, so only the butt and back legs are in the water.
4. Swish the water around soiled area. You can gently pick away the poop once it has softened, but not while dry. Pulling can injury the bunny's fragile skin.
5. Dry thoroughly by sitting bunny on towel and patting butt with towel and paper towels until dry. A hair dryer on very low heat may be needed, but not too hot.

Dry Butt Bath Method

1. Start with pure Baby Cornstarch Powder. Do not use ANY powder that contains talc. Talc can cause respiratory issues, among other problems.
2. Make sure your bunny is comfortably placed on towels and the soiled areas are easily accessible.
3. Apply cornstarch to the soiled areas and work gently into fur.
4. The cornstarch will help "release" the debris from the fur.
5. You may need to use a comb or brush to remove the smaller bits of remaining debris, but please do this gently. A bunny's skin can actually tear easily.

The House Rabbit Society website has a video demonstrating the proper way to give your bunny a safe butt bath. www.rabbit.org

Chewing

Bunnies not only like to chew things, they NEED to chew things. Their teeth are constantly growing. Cardboard boxes are great and inexpensive to give a bunny. A bunny will chew and dig in a box until they get it the way they want it. This is called "bunstruction" in the bunny world. Please make sure there aren't any staples or loose tape for your bunny to ingest in the box.

 Finn loves to chew his way through a good box.

You can see more of his bunstruction projects by following Cin & Finn on Facebook.

Photo courtesy of Cindy Trivette

Not having plenty of hay or chew toys can cause a bunny's teeth to become overgrown, grow at an angle, or develop spurs, all requiring medical treatment. These types of dental problems are very painful and will cause a bunny to stop eating. Bunnies must eat all the time to keep their insides healthy and working properly. A bunny savvy veterinarian will always check your bunny's teeth during an exam. As you can see, having items to chew on is very important to the health and well-being of your bunny.

Ezra is a Master Shredder of all things he can reach. Bunnies are very helpful at chewing anything they believe needs it. If you don't think it needs to be chewed, you might want to put it out of bunny's reach.

Photo courtesy of Linda Culbert

Mr. Binks enjoys a good bunny-safe wooden toy to chew and throw around. Make sure the toys you choose for your bunny are actually for bunnies. There are many so-called bunny toys on the market that actually are not safe.

Photo courtesy of Jennifer MacLaughlin

Jackpot envisioned a window in his box, so he watched some Do It Yourself videos on YouTube and immediately got to work on the project. There is no stopping a bunny on a mission. It's up to you to choose whether the window will be on a box or your wallpaper.

Photo courtesy of Debrah Smith

Destructive

Bunnies can be very destructive, especially if they are bored. It is important to give them things that are okay to destroy. Bunny-proof your home with gates, exercise pens, cable protective tubing, or by putting things away.

Cami's surgical talent.

Cami ~ Photos courtesy of Katie Cohee

Popular items bunnies may destroy:

- Any power cord or wiring
- Baseboards
- Carpet
- Shoes
- Clothing
- Blankets
- Remote Control buttons
- Everything else

BunBun is an overachiever! Good thing she's cute! Photo courtesy of Joe LaCaille and Desi Hawkins

Sunshine took it upon herself to help her family start the floor remodeling job. Of course, Sunshine might be the reason for the floor remodeling job.

Some bunnies really love to dig and chew carpet.

Proof of Sunshine's talent (left).

Photos courtesy of Brenda Shirley

Destroyed carpet courtesy of Sunshine

Pickles (right) enjoys digging and shredding a phonebook. It's messy, but much less destructive and expensive than carpet or furniture or walls or....

Follow Pickles and friends on Instagram at gangster.rabbits

Photo courtesy of Janna Blaydes

Most phonebooks are printed with soy-based ink, making them bunny-safe. If your bunny actually eats the phonebook, obviously your bunny is not a good candidate for having it.

Try sprinkling pellets between pages to keep your bunny busy and to slow down his or her eating.

Ears

Never pick up a bunny by their ears. You can severely injure and scare your bunny. In fact, most bunnies don't like to be picked up at all. If you do, pick them up by placing your arm underneath their belly and supporting their legs and back. Bunnies can kick hard enough to actually break their back.

Duck is actually not a duck, he's a bunny. A gorgeous bunny with magnificent ears.

Photo courtesy of Linda Culbert

Sterling (above) can hear a banana being peeled from a mile away!

Photo courtesy of Stephanie Gould

Hazel B (right) looks sweet and lovable, but she can throw down a tantrum and show her mom the error of her ways.

Follow Hazel on Facebook at Hazel the Fluffy Bun

Photo courtesy of Colleen Deafenbaugh

Gracie with her soft, angelic lop ears keep her out of trouble.

Photo courtesy of Julie Barb

Holly has her ears set for just the right frequency to hear the treat bag.

Photo courtesy of Julie Barb

Pint-sized Oreo demands attention from mom, Gretta Parker, author of The $7.50 Bunny That Changed the World and founder of the Flopsy Parker Memorial Sanctuary.

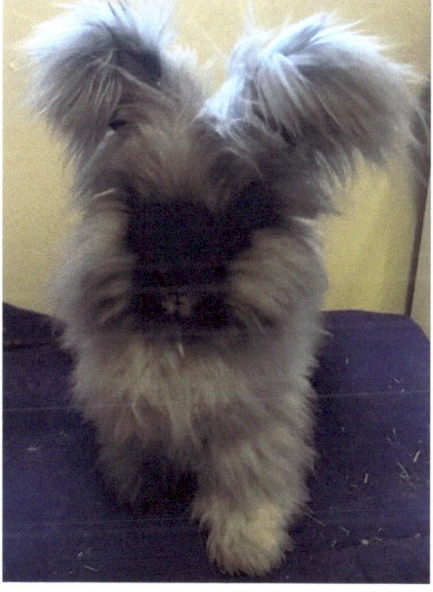

Addie's ears almost don't look real, they are so perfect. But they are real and they hear everything, especially the treat bag.

Photo courtesy of Sandra Lee

Friends

Bunnies are social animals and need a friend. However, it doesn't always have to be another bunny. It can be a well behaved dog, cat, or human.

Capone and his dog friend, Saya, love hanging out together. Saya is very gentle with her bunny siblings. Not all dogs are, so please use caution. Their human mom is a dog trainer.

Follow Capone on Instagram at

gangster.rabbits

Photo courtesy of Janna Blaydes..

It's all about teamwork with Suzie and Kramer (below). ~Tracy Meadows

Fred & Barney are 5 1/2 year old brothers, who are inseparable. They do everything together, including begging mom for treats. They seem to be in sync with "the stare."

Photo courtesy of Michelle Zeman, author of Chronicles of a Wererabbit.

L-R
Peanut B
Watson
and
Sweetpea

Follow this adorable trio on Facebook at Sweetpea, Peanut B and Watson: Much loved buns   Photo courtesy of Tracey Heaton

Sterling and his feline brother, Kyle like to hang out together and wait for their human sister to drop snacks. With a toddler, the possibilities are endless!

Photo courtesy of   Stephanie Gould

L-R: Ana, Ginger, Princess Flop, Jori, Dolly, and Fjora can be followed on Instagram @mariesbunnies. I mean, why would you not want follow these adorable bunnies? Seriously, why not?   Photo courtesy of Marie Starr.

Grooming

Bunnies are generally very clean animals, but they do require help from humans. Bunnies molt (shed) a few times a year, alternating between light and heavy molting periods, and it can last up to six weeks. Bunnies groom like cats, but cannot throw up hairballs like cats. The more fur you can remove, the better chance your bunny has at not developing a blockage from ingested fur. Bunnies also need regular nail trimmings and their teeth need checked for problems.

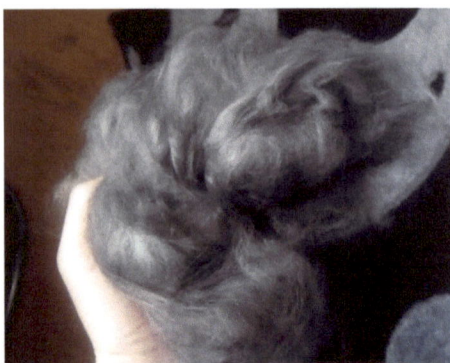

This is Leo (left) and this is the fur that came off of him in just one brushing. You can see why brushing is so important for your bunny.

Photo courtesy of Erin Nypaver

If you look closely at Betsy (right), you can see the shed pattern towards her backside. Bunnies have very thin skin, so you want to gently brush, comb, or pluck this fur. Betsy is groomed regularly, so don't be alarmed if your well-groomed bunny surprises you with a super-molt one day.

Betsy's mom will often groom her outdoors. *You'll notice Betsy is wearing a leash for her own safety. She is always supervised and she's in her own non-chemically treated yard.

Photo courtesy of Jenn Eckert

Follow Jenn's bunnies at Rabbitat for Humanity-Therapy Buns on Both Sides of the Bridge

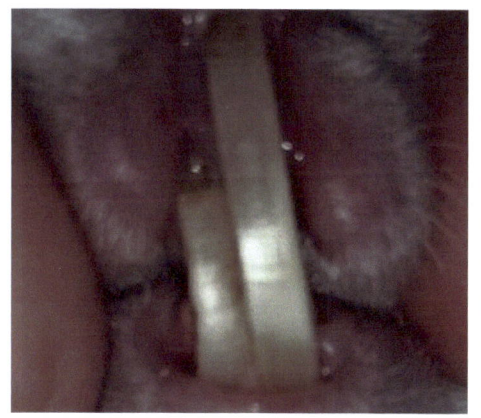

These teeth belong to a bunny who came into a rescue. They are overgrown and the gums are inflamed. Thankfully, this bunny received the medical attention and the love it needed to live a healthy, happy life.

Teeth problems will quickly cause a bunny to stop eating, often leading to very serious or fatal problems.

Photo courtesy of Linda Culbert

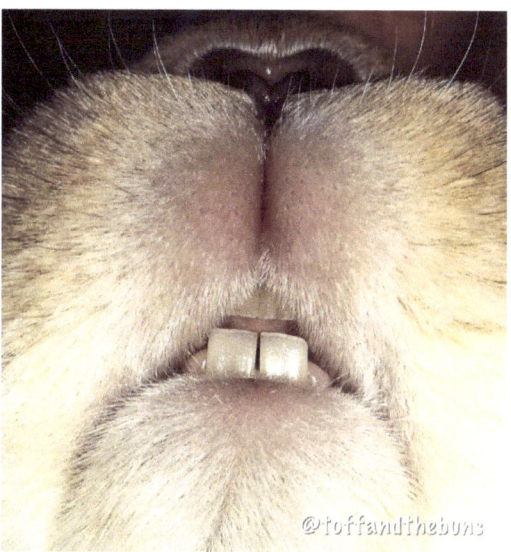

Alfred (right) is proud of his perfectly shaped pearly whites and he should be, they are fantastic!

Chewing hay and bunny safe chew toys helps keep teeth filed down. Pellets can help, but pellets should be a very small percent of your bunny's diet. So plenty of hay and chew toys are a necessity. A veterinarian may sometimes need to file your bunny's teeth.

Follow Alfred at toffandthebuns on Instagram.

Photo courtesy of Angie Hutson

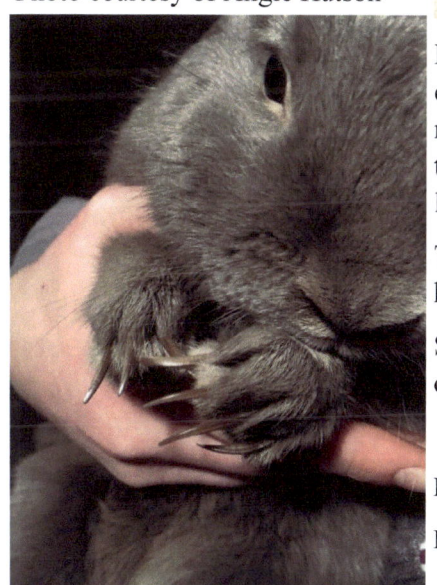

Most bunnies do not like having a manicure, and they will let you know it. For this reason, many people take their bunny to the vet for a nail trimming. It's usually less stressful for everyone involved.

The House Rabbit Society has an excellent how-to video on nail trimming.

See back of back for more details and tips on nail trimming

Photo courtesy of Michelle Koopman-Miller

E.A.R.S. Eerie Area Rabbit Society & Rescue

Herbs

Herbs fall into two categories in the fresh leafy green portion of a bunny's diet. Herbs/Greens that fall into Leafy Greens I category are higher in Oxalic Acid. These should only be fed once a day, and should be on a rotation. Herbs/Greens in the Leafy Greens II category are acceptable to feed daily. See a more complete list in the back of this book.

Suzie, posing with her basil plant, right before throwing it and eating it.

Xander enjoying his mint in the privacy of his box. Follow Xander on Facebook at Xander Magneto.   Photo courtesy of Vannissa Kraemer

Sophia is pretty serious about her cilantro and getting it into her mouth.   Photo courtesy of Jennifer MacLaughlin

Hedley (right) is gulping down some parsley like he hasn't eaten a thing in weeks. Coincidently this is how most bunnies eat.

Parsley is one of the herbs in the Leafy Greens I category, so it shouldn't be eaten more than once a day and should be rotated with other greens. You will find more information in the back of this book.

Photo courtesy of Raven Taylor

Murphy (left) stuffing his adorable face with carrot tops. Although, carrots are not an herb, I just had to find a good spot in this book for this happy muncher. The tops can be fed like any other Herb/Green. The actual carrot should be fed sparling due to sugar content.

Follow Murphy and his friends on Facebook at Hoppel, Maila & Murphy

Photo courtesy of Alexa Cammann

Theo and Darla (right) enjoy a nice spread of flat parsley (Leafy Green I) mixed with some organic kale (Leafy Green II).

Follow this adorable couple on Instagram at

TheoandDarlaPhoto courtesy of Kate Faust

Intelligent

Bunnies are very intelligent animals. They know the sound of their favorite treat bag, the fridge door being opened, and basically anything else resembling a treat. They also know how to telepathically communicate with humans to get what they want. Basically means staring at the human or looking cute until the human notices and gives in.

In Luigi's spare time, he likes to study up on things like Surgical Diagnosis. His dad might want to make sure he doesn't serve meals late.

Follow Luigi on Facebook at Luigi the Bunny.

Photos courtesy of Johnny Vidster.

Walter and Betsy quickly mastered their treat/food dispenser like pros! Bunnies are so food and treat driven that it can often work to your advantage. Of course, they can also be quite demanding about it, too.

A dispenser like this can also be used for bunnies who need to slow down their eating, due to being overweight or as a choking precaution. Betsy's mom has had to save her from choking and I have had to do the same with Suzie. It's very scary.

Alfie looks like a CEO on his way to a board meeting, but he's actually working on his manners and learning how to one day become a therapy bunny like his predecessors, Walter P. and Betsy Eckert .

Photos courtesy of Jenn Eckert

Follow Jenn's bunnies at

Rabbitat for Humanity-Therapy Buns on Both Sides of the Bridge

Jump

When bunnies feel exceptionally happy, they will run laps and jump in the air. Jumping is actually called 'binkies' in bunny language. They just randomly jump in the air. They may be running at the time, or even sitting still. It's like an uncontrollable "thing" that takes over. Good luck getting a clear picture of one, though.

Davos (top left) and Tiana (top right)

Amanda might be one of the luckiest people to get the number of "binkies" she gets on camera. She's obviously doing something right for so many bunnies in her care to be so happy. She has her own bunnies and also fosters through Against All Odds Rabbit Rescue. Visit this group on Facebook for more adorable bunny pictures.

Photos courtesy of Amanda Greening

Dixon (bottom left) and Jabberwocky (bottom right)

Khaleesi (top left) and Tyrion (top right) are fan favorites.

Photos courtesy of Amanda Greening

Sophia loves to binky all over the house. She also likes smiling.

Photos courtesy of Jennifer MacLaughlin

Jennifer volunteers for Tranquility Animal Trail Sanctuary, fosters for the Humane Society, and is always on-call for her own bunnies.

Kisses

You have already read about the bunny attitude, but bunnies can also be very affectionate with other bunnies, humans, or other pets, and they might even show their affection with kisses. Suzie charges for her kisses.

Kwyn and Watson (below) love each other. Photo courtesy of Amanda Greening.

Rex gives his human mom kisses every day. Their favorite time together is in the morning while his mom is drinking her coffee. Rex joins her for some mom/bunny quiet time. Follow Rex on Facebook at Rex the Bunny

Photo courtesy of Carolina Massie

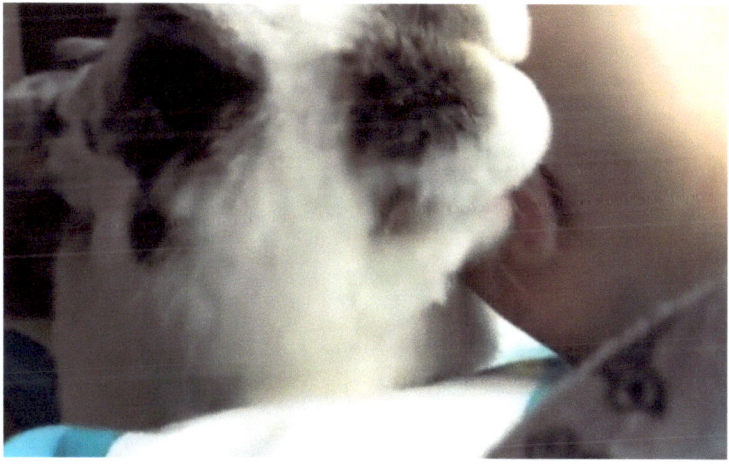

It was no accident that this little ones name is Sweetie. She IS a sweetheart. Follow Sweetie on Facebook at The Residents of Fairy Castle Farm

Photo courtesy of Yollie Boag

Litter box

Can bunnies be litter trained? Absolutely! They actually love their litter box, but they do require some training. A spayed or neutered bunny is generally easier to train. Every bunny is different. So finding the right type of litter and litter box may take a few tries. Facebook bunny groups and rescue groups are often a good place to ask what others use for their bunnies.

I line Suzie's litter box with newspaper, add a very thin layer of Feline Pine Pellets to soak up the urine, and then cover it with hay. I add a handful of fresh hay on top daily. She likes to sleep in her litter box, so this also helps to keep her clean and fresh.

- Never use dusty, scoopable, or clay-type cat litter. These types can irritate eyes, cause respiratory problems, and cause a fatal blockage if eaten.

- Never use pine or cedar shavings. The phenols in the shavings can be very toxic and may cause liver damage in small animals.

- Wood pellets, like Feline Pine, are kiln dried, which removes most phenols and oils.

- Yesterday's News and Carefresh (name brand) are both good. Keep an eye on any change of ingredients, like baking soda for example.

Snowy's mom likes to use straw on top of her wood pellets and then add hay on one end. This creates a nice cushion while Snowy is eating. The straw doesn't soak up the urine, but it directs it to the wood pellets below.

Photo courtesy of Cindy Sanchez

Moshi and Marlee do everything together. They eat, sleep, and even go to the litter box together. Cathie uses a litter screen she purchased through the Binky Bunny online store. It's a flexible, hardware cloth, which is easier on bunny feet versus a stiff cover. The special screen sits right on top of the litter. It's best to spread a little hay over the screen for extra cushion for their feet.

The screen serves multiple purposes: If you have a digger, this will help keep the litter IN the box; prevents the dirty litter from getting mixed with the clean litter, so you don't have to change out the whole box as often; and if you compost, the hay and poop are on top of the screen, not mixed in with litter.

Photo and screen explanation courtesy of Cathie Jackson

When Suzie goes out to an event, like MidWest Bunfest, she travels with a small litter box inside the stroller. It's like a portable potty for her. It also seems to make her feel relaxed and more secure. She munches on hay while people pet her. Of course, since she's in her litter box, she is likely also pooping while being petted, but that's her little secret….. Well, maybe not anymore. Sorry Suzie, your secret is out.

Follow Suzie on Facebook at The Bossy Bunny.

Messy

Bunnies seem like they would be clean, well-mannered animals, but bring one into your home and you will quickly discover just how messy they are. It can be disheartening to spend time cleaning and arranging your bunny's area. You think it looks perfect and imagine how much your bunny will love it, only to find out you did it all wrong. Your bunny immediately starts trashing his or her area the moment you turn your back. Welcome to life with a house rabbit.

Christopher (right) and his human have different ideas of what "neat" actually means.

Picture courtesy of Liz Incardone

I first saw the picture on the left as an Easter Public Service Announcement. I wonder how many people would get bunnies on a whim, if they saw this picture of Cupcake's decorating skills?

Photo courtesy of Janna Blaydes

Angel (right) obviously has no use for a nice, clean blanket or nice, clean anything for that matter. What an angel…..

Photo courtesy of Kim Benge

Ava might look like a princess, but she parties like a rock star!

Photo courtesy of Marielle Sarkan

Jackpot likes to help his human with her exercise by spreading his mess around as much as possible.   Photo courtesy of Debrah Smith

Noisy

Most people think bunnies are polite, quiet little animals. Anyone who shares a home with a bunny knows how untrue that notion really is. They make noises when happy, sad, mad, or bored. They make noises with their feet, with their mouths, and by rattling, shaking, or throwing things.

You know when a bunny uses the power of the thump, that they are not impressed with you nor whatever it is you are doing to annoy them. This can be something you are actually doing, like cleaning out their area, or even something they think you might do.

Rogger (left) has perfect foot-thumping feet and he knows how to use them.

Photo courtesy of Jackie Horalek

Francis and Shipley (right) are not pleased that they had to be blocked from the carpet cleaning activities. So, Shipley rattled her gate until she was set free. Rattling their cage or pen endlessly is highly effective.

Visit Uptown Bunny on Facebook, where their motto is, "A tiny store with big dreams of making bunnies binky!" You'll find items for bunnies and bunny people there.

Photos courtesy of

Kim Maring

Occupied

Bunnies need things to occupy them. If you don't give them something safe to keep them busy, they will find something themselves. Unfortunately what they find might not be so desirable for you or it could be something dangerous to your bunny.

Finn likes to bowl in his "spare" time. He also enjoys long walks on the beach and hiking in the mountains. Okay, not really, but you get the idea.

Photo courtesy of Cindy Trivette. Follow Finn on Facebook at Cin & Finn

Gypsy plays hard and naps hard. She loves rearranging her cups. And by rearranging, I mean, she likes to throw her cups. Sometimes she will even throw them over her head.

She is currently in the bonding process with a new friend, Harley, so she is spends a lot of time checking out her stuff to make sure he hasn't gotten any boy germs on anything belonging to her..

Photo courtesy of Deb Jacobs

For great bunny tested and bunny approved toys, check out Bunderland Bunny Toy Emporium on Etsy.

Every toy is handcrafted for small animals to safely chew, toss, and enrich their lives.

Daisy is doing amazing work heading up Ocean's Army. To de-stress from her obligations, she likes throw her toys around and then nap. You can follow Daisy on Ocean's Facebook page. Photo courtesy of Sue O'Reilly

Checkers is checking out his temporary housing with Triangle Rabbit Rescue (TRR), while he waits for his forever home.

TRR is a North Carolina chapter of the House Rabbit Society.

Visit Triangle Rabbits at www.TriangleRabbits.org and on Facebook.

Poop

Bunnies can be litter box trained. However, even the best trained bunny may still leave a few dropping around at times. Bunnies are also very territorial, and this is one way they like to mark their territory. Suzie likes to leave her poop markings in the cat beds at our house.

You can thank Suzie for this perfect pile of poop. These droppings are perfect for her size. They aren't too soft or too dry. This means she is eating a lot of hay and drinking a lot of water.

Suzie always knew her poop was special, but she had no idea how special this type of poop really is. Or maybe she does and that's why she doesn't like me to steal it.

You can tell so much about your bunny's health just by learning the difference in his/her poop. If you've ever had a sick bunny, you know how important it is to examine your bunny's poop, especially if you haven't seen any within a few hours.

When you see a "string of pearls" type of poop, it means your bunny is ingesting fur. Brushing will help prevent the ingested fur from becoming a blockage. Bunnies cannot throw up, so it is imperative that you brush or pluck the loose fur from your bunny. Unlimited hay and water also help to push the ingested fur through the digestive system.

Both of these poop samples are from Suzie. You can see how much smaller the one on the left is. She wasn't eating enough hay, so I started providing her with a variety of hay and you can see how much larger the poop on the right is. Good job, Suzie!

Soft, moist dropping usually mean your bunny's diet is to high in protein or sugar. Try decreasing these foods and increasing the hay intake. If these types of droppings still continue, you may need to check with your veterinarian to make sure there isn't something else going on with your bunny's health.

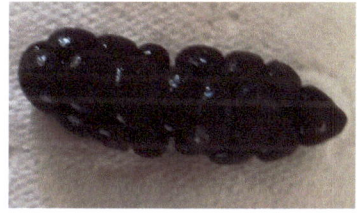

Small clusters of shiny droppings that look like a blackberry or a bunch of grapes is technically not considered poop. It is called cecotropes or cecal pellets. They are quite smelly and mushy, but they are common. There is a healthy bacteria in these smelly gems and it is very important that your bunny re-ingest these (yes, eat them). If you see an excessive amount of these lying around, take a look at your bunny's diet. You might need to scale the treats and pellets back a bit. Be prepared for your approval rating to go down, though.

Photos courtesy of Amie Seal (and Kevin, left)

The word "cecotropes" doesn't really roll off the tongue, no pun intended. Many people have their own name for it. We call them butt snacks at our house, but I've seen bum nuggets, bum toffees, poopcicles, butt candy, butt butter, etc.

Here is Suzie demonstrating "the pose" while under my desk at work one day. Butt snacks *are* portable.

Quirky

Bunnies can be quiet, calm, and peaceful to watch sleep. They can also be down right comical. Bunnies do all sorts of quirky things that make you shake your head and laugh.

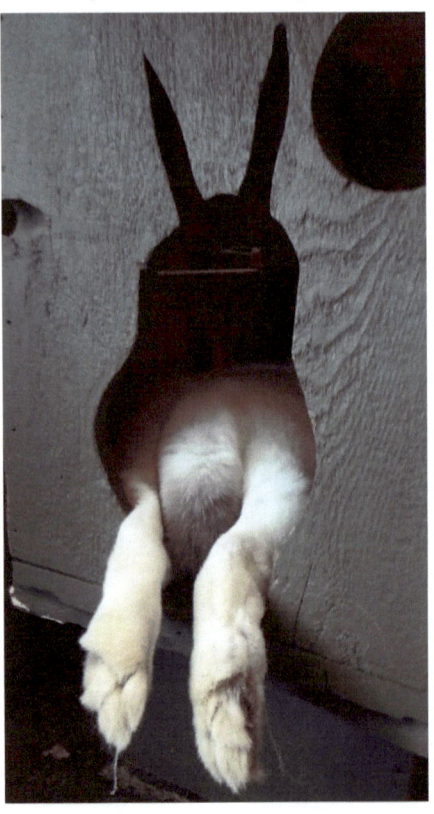

Bob and Marley (above) are very large, gentle goofballs.

Photo courtesy of Lindsey Campbell

Alice and kids (below) uhhh….

Photo courtesy of Taiya Holden

Roxy (above and below) "hiding" in her hide-a-way.

Photo courtesy of Tammy Danoff

Thumps (above) was *really* enjoying whatever he was eating. Have you ever seen such a long tongue on a bunny?!?!

Follow Thumps and his friend, Bonbon, on Instagram at rex_and_chex

Photo courtesy of Stephanie Pabst

Have you ever seen your bunny rub his or her chin on something? This is known as "chinning it." It now belongs to the bunny. Sterling is demonstrating how to chin something. The wall is now his.

Photo courtesy of Stephanie Gould

Suzie likes to throw her empty bowls down the ramp of her cottage when she's finished eating breakfast.

Violet doesn't seem fully committed to the rooftop nap.

Michael Adamowski

Research

Doing your research before bringing a bunny into your home is very important. If you have a bunny, you already know they are not low-maintenance pets. If this book is your introduction to bunnies, and you've made it to this page, then you've likely learned that they are not what you expected.

Suzie, squeezing in a quick nap while doing her research.

The more you learn about bunnies, the happier and healthier your bunny will be, and the happier you will be. Learning the early warning signs that your bunny is sick can save your bunny's life and maybe even save you a few dollars. Money saved can be used to buy your bunny more toys , treats, and hay!

When Suzie isn't busy working on our website or Facebook page for The Bossy Bunny, she enjoys catching up on House Rabbit Society news. She's likely waiting for the treats list to be updated to include more blueberries per serving.

Our website is dedicated to education on bunny care. We like it to be kid-friendly, as there are many kids with bunnies, who need to learn how to properly care for them.

www.TheBossyBunny.com

There are several Facebook pages, websites, and blogs dedicated to bunny health and welfare. The House Rabbit Society (HRS) is our favorite go-to website for everything rabbit.

The HRS was founded in 1988 and is the only International rabbit rescue and educational organization.

There are chapters and educators in many states in the U.S., plus Canada, Australia, and Italy. They are always expanding their outreach, in hopes of helping more rabbits.

One of my favorite things about the HRS website, is the huge list of short, education videos made by HRS Vice President, Mary Cotter, and Actress/Comedian/HRS Educator, Amy Sedaris. The videos are not just educational, but quite enjoyable to watch. You will find dozens of helpful videos on their site, including nail trimming, litter box training, brushing (bunnies have VERY delicate skin), rabbit proofing your home, bonding bunnies, giving belly massages to relieve gas (which can be very dangerous in bunnies), and the list goes on.

You will even find a list of bunny-savvy veterinarians in your area on the HRS website.

www.Rabbit.org

Snacks

Bunnies LOVE snacks and will go to any measure to get what they want. If you buy commercially made bunny treats, please check the ingredients. Not all treats are actually healthy or safe for your bunny. Bananas are also good for disguising medication. No seeds, nuts, or corn. Ever!

Jerry and Panda (left) go bonkers over bananas.

Photo courtesy of Tarza Taimur

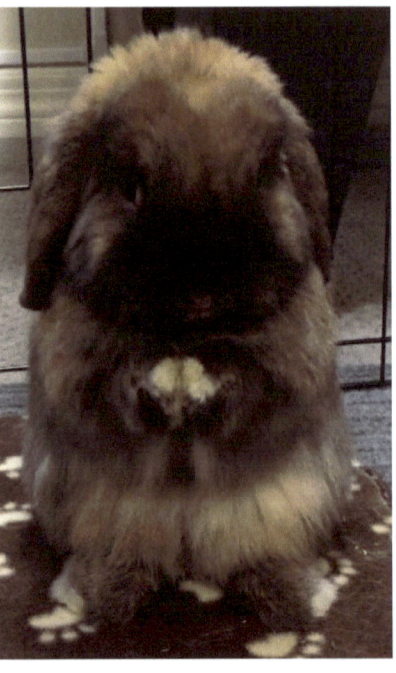

Mr. Binks (above) is always in begging mode. He knows how it works.

Photo courtesy of

Jennifer MacLauglin

Malcolm and Mr. Beans share a banana. Mr. Beans also likes to make a fashion statement.

Follow these boys on their Facebook page, Mr. Beans & Friends.

Photo courtesy of Kaitlen Rose Scott

Fruits should only be given as a treat and in very small quantities, as they can be very sugary.

Fruit shouldn't be more than 1 teaspoon per 2 pounds of body weight per day.

The House Rabbit Society has a full list of fruits on their website, including proper portions.

Rocky (left) gets very serious over blueberries.

Photo courtesy of Carla Renee

Bunnies have also been known to steal a treat or two, like Softie (below). They are sneaky! Follow Softie on Facebook at We LOVE Softie. Photo courtesy of Tarza Taimur

Tunnels

Bunnies love tunnels! They love exploring, hiding, and running in and out of tthem. You can see below that Suzie has quite an assortment of tunnels, not including the one in her area. The cat section at most chain stores and online stores often have tunnels.

You can find tunnels made from cardboard, wicker, or even timothy hay, all great for chewing, as well. You can even get creative with boxes and make your own tunnels.

Penelope and Hoptimus Prime (above) enjoy sharing some quiet time in their new tunnel. Photo courtesy of Dawn Haggerty

Sunny (above) especially enjoys a model with a sunroof.

Photo courtesy of Deb Jacobs

Violet (above) reassures Buddy (in tunnel) that, no, mom will never find you hiding in this tunnel.

Photo courtesy of Carla Renee

The tunnel above allows you to lengthen or shorten it, curve it or straighten it. Very versatile.

Suzie (above) trying out for a part on the next James Bond movie.

Unlimited Hay and Water

There is nothing more important in a bunny's diet than hay and water. Bunnies should have access to both at all times. Hay helps keep teeth healthy and bunny's insides working properly.

Sherlock (left) is shocked to learn that hay should be 80% of his daily diet. He always thought bananas should be 80%.

Follow Sherlock on Instagram at Sherlock.the.bunny

Photo courtesy of Hatka

Hrebendova

Try a variety of good grass hays like: Timothy, Orchard, Oat Hay, or Brome.

Alfalfa hay is not a grass hay, but a legume. It is higher in calories and protein. Most often used for very young or elderly bunnies who need the extra calories.

Annie (right) was rescued and in foster care when this picture was taken. Oftentimes, a mouthful of hay like Annie has is a nesting sign, even if the bunny is spayed, they will still do this.

Photo courtesy of Misti Roe

No such thing as personal space when it comes to this hay time for this adorable foursome.

L-R: Erik, Scotty, Dandy, and Bobby

Photo courtesy of Rebecca Campbell

Princess (below) can hardly wait for a new shipment of hay to arrive. She just hops on into the box.

Follow Princess and Marcie on their Facebook page at Lemmon Buns.

Photo courtesy of Becky Lemmon

Christopher (above) is working really hard at getting in the 80% hay portion of his diet, so he can beg for treats.

Photo courtesy of Liz Incardone

Unlimited Water

Having access to fresh water at all times is very important to a bunny's digestive system. They can become dehydrated very quickly and die, if they don't drink enough water.

Drinking from a heavy bowl is the preferred method by bunnies and their humans. Some bunnies do have a tendency to flip their bowls or run through them, making the placement of the bowl tricky. You can buy a bowl that will attach to the side of the pen wall. Suzie used to make a mess with her water bowl, so I put a large heavy bowl inside a small, clean litter box and used a towel to stuff in between the bowl and sides of the litter box. It kept the bowl in place and soaked up the water. Suzie no longer needs the box or towel now.

Vegetables and Greens

You already know that hay should be 80% of your bunny's diet. The other 20% should be made up of fresh leafy greens, vegetables, and fruit. See below for a short list of the fresh portion breakdown:

- 75% should come from a variety of leafy green lettuces like red, green, or Romaine, but never Iceberg. Arugula, carrot tops, kale, and dandelion greens are just a few other examples.
- 15% of the fresh foods portion should be non-leafy vegetables like celery (without the stringy fiber), summer squash, bell peppers, and zucchini.
- 10% (maximum) of the fresh foods portion should be fruit, like berries and apple, but many fruits are high in sugar and should be used as a treat.

Portions are based on 2 pounds per body weight: 1 packed cup of leafy greens; 1 tablespoon of non-leafy vegetables; and 1 teaspoon of fruit. This list is for an average bunny over a year old. Like people, not all bunnies can eat the same foods, due to special needs, age, or stomach sensitivity.

Visit the House Rabbit Society for a more complete list of foods and suggestions.

www.Rabbit.org

Shamrock, Valentino, and Pumpkin (left) enjoy a nice salad together. Hope the salad wasn't served late! We know the attitude Pumpkin is capable of having.

Photo courtesy of Justina Hoflock

Follow Sweetie, Angel, and Teegee on Facebook at The Residents of Fairy Castle Farm. Photo courtesy of Yollie Bloag.

Lucky & Mandi (left) enjoy napping, snooping, and eating together. They spend all of their time posing and looking adorable for their mom's camera. More photos equals more treats.

Photo courtesy of Kathy Pappas.

If you are going to feed your bunny pellets, be sure to look for ones that are at least an 18% fiber timothy pellet and do not include colorful pieces in them.

Wild Rabbits

The wild rabbits you see outdoors may look like domestic rabbits, but they are actually a different species. Their needs are different and their life span is much shorter. Many people think the impulse-buy rabbit they bought would be better off outdoors, but they couldn't be more wrong. The life-span for a wild rabbit isn't much more than a year at best, while a domestic rabbit can have a life-span of 8-12 years.

There are several species of wild rabbits in the U.S. Some wild rabbits dig deep burrows, while others, like the Cottontail, make a more shallow dip for nesting. This is why it is very important to check your yard before mowing. Babies are only in the nest for a few weeks, so be patient and they will move on without your help.

Photos courtesy of Alicia Hodgson, who works for a wildlife hospital.

If you find a nest of abandoned baby bunnies in your yard, they are most likely not abandoned. Mom only comes around at dusk and/or dawn to feed them. She does this to keep them safe by not drawing attention to them.

The above leafy greens were being grown for a house rabbit, but it also got the attention of a wild rabbit. Wild rabbits do like to help themselves to your garden, so be prepared to share.

Photo courtesy of Kingsley Keiko

If you find an injured baby, please contact a wildlife hospital or rehabber. Bunnies are very fragile, especially babies. The likelihood of a baby bunny surviving in your care is very slim. Rehabbers have permits with special training, and usually medical contacts for wildlife. Your regular veterinarian likely cannot legally tend to wildlife. I would suggest looking up the local number for the wildlife hospital and rescuers in your area and keep the information in your phone and/or wallet. In the event of an emergency, every second counts.

In fact, add the number here, in your book, so you will be reminded of it.

Local wildlife hospital: Phone: _____

Email: _____

Website: _____

Local wildlife rehabber Contact: _____

X-pen

Bunnies need room to stretch and play. A small cage is just not enough . You can find an exercise pen online for a really good price. You can even add extra panels. Be sure to get one tall enough so your bunny can't jump out. Remember, bunnies all need time outside of their pen daily to run around and explore.

Pictured left is a basic setup. You can add toys, tunnels, and boxes to keep them entertained.

Photo courtesy of Jennifer MacLaughlin and her foster bunny (pictured)

Fern likes to move the x-pen around in different shapes for her bunnies. Checking out every new corner keeps them busy. Pictured below is Suki (left) and Arabella (right).   Follow Fern's bunnies on Instagram @ arabella.suki.alanis   Photo courtesy of Fern Casey Que

Above is Kennedy (black) and Missy (black and white). They have an enclosure made out of customizable pet playpen panels. You can get really creative with these individual pieces. Obviously this cute duo approves (see below).

Follow Kennedy and Missy on Facebook at Les amis/ es de Kennedy at Missy.

Photo courtesy of Sandrine Marquis

Another way to use an x-pen is to stretch it out and block off areas you don't want your bunny to have access to aka bunny proofing.

Abraham (right) is likely to already have an escape plan.

Photo courtesy of Debrah Smith

Yawn

Yes, bunnies do yawn, but it is a rare sight. While some people seem to witness the bunny yawn often, many others never will. I've had Suzie almost four years yet, as I write this book, I have never seen her yawn. If you get to see it, you are one of the lucky few.

I am bunny! Hear me R O A R!!!

Follow Theo (above) on Instagram at TheoAndDarla

Photo courtesy of Kate Faust

Looks like Softie (left) is singing the praises of his human, and he should be! Softie is a very fortunate rescue bunny who lives in Iraq, with his human, Tarza.

Tarza has very few resources available to her, including rabbit savvy veterinarians or medications to help keep bunnies healthy. The work Tarza is doing with such little resources is truly amazing.

Follow this adorable bunny and the work that Tarza is doing on Facebook at We LOVE Softie.

Thank you for what you do, Tarza!

Photo courtesy of Tarza Taimur

Valentino (right) looks as though he is screaming, "Let me out of here! I swear, I'm innocent! I didn't steal the bananas you left on the table!." But he is really just settling in for yet his fifteenth nap of the day.

Photo courtesy of Justina Hoflock

Zonked

Bunnies come in all shapes and sizes, with all types of personalities, but one thing they all have in common….they look adorable when they are sleeping.

Christopher (above) is all tucked in for the night.
Photo courtesy of Liz Incardone

When a bunny gets as relaxed as Eeyore, (above) it can create a moment of panic while you check to make sure the bunny is still breathing. They can get pretty relaxed.   Photo courtesy of Brenda Shirley

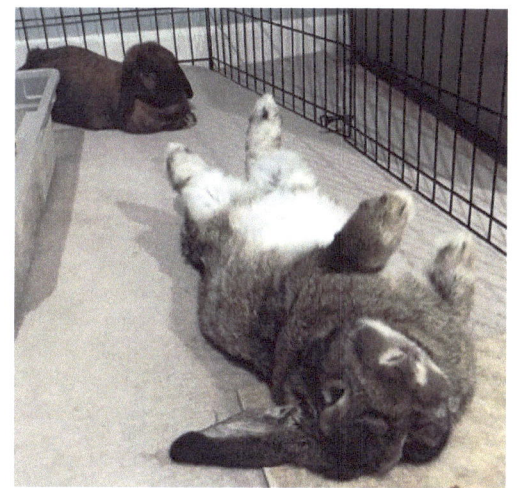

Darla (in background) watches on while Theo totally zonks out. Theo is a bit dramatic in everything he does.

Follow these two on Instagram at

TheoAndDarla

Photo courtesy of Kate Faust

Suzie (above) and Mr. Binks (above right) prefer to face melt into the floor.

Mr. Binks photo courtesy of Jennifer MacLaughlin

Walter (left) and Betsy (right) rarely sleep, one without the other.

Follow Rabbitat for Humanity-Therapy Buns from Both Sides of the Bridge on Facebook.   Photo courtesy of Jenn Eckert

Appendix

Vegetables continued

Natasha's Story

Health and Wellness Tips

The Life of an Easter Bunny review

Special Thanks and Photo Credits

This list is continued from the Vegetables pages and based on the list found on the House Rabbit Society website. Not all bunnies like or can eat the same foods, due to an illness or stomach sensitivity. **It's important that you know what works for your own bunny.** For example, Suzie has eaten broccoli stems for years, yet other bunnies can't eat it without getting sick. Always introduce new foods slowly.

Leafy Greens I	Leafy Greens II		Non-Leafy Vegetables
(choose one & rotate)	(choose two)	Mint	
Parsley	Arugula	Basil	Broccoli leaves & stems
Spinach	Carrot Tops	Cilantro	Celery cut into pieces
Mustard Greens	Dandelion Greens	Dill Leaves	Carrots (small amount due to sugar content)
Radish Tops	Kale	Fennel (the leafy tops and the base)	
	Red Lettuce		Brussels Sprouts
(Leafy Greens from this list are higher in oxalic acid)	Green Lettuce	Watercress	Edible Flowers (roses, pansies, hibiscus)
	Romaine Lettuce	Wheatgrass	

FRUITS

Apple	Mango
Apricot	Melons
Banana (no peel)	Pear
Berries (any type)	No stems, seeds, or pits. The peel is nutritious, unless otherwise noted.
Cherries	

54

Natasha's Rescue

Natasha's story probably started out like so many other bunnies before her. Someone decided a bunny was too much work and dumped her to fiend for herself. Not all bunnies dumped outdoors have a happy ending. Luckily this is Natasha's story and it does have a happy ending, a true rags to riches ending.

Natasha was eating grass out in the open on a busy corner. Grass that was likely treated with pesticides. She was living in bamboo. She didn't know enough to hide from predators. Her snowy white fur made her a very visible target for anything or anyone. Luckily she caught the eye of a bunny lover who knew a seasoned bunny rescuer, Liz.

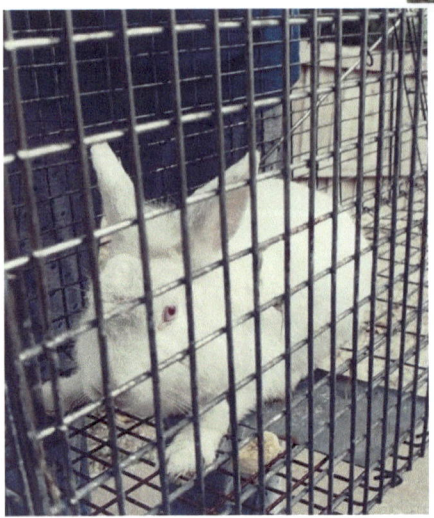

Over the years, Liz has trapped several bunnies by using the exercise (x-pen) method, which is where the bunny is lured into an open pen. Once the bunny goes inside, you bring the open ends together, trapping the bunny inside. After more than a week, it was obvious this girl wasn't going to be trapped with a pen. A humane Havahart trap had to be set up and as you can see, it worked! You have to make sure the trap is closely monitored and not left unattended for long periods of time.

Once captured, Natasha was taken to a veterinarian. The diagnosis wasn't good in the beginning. She had an upper respiratory infection (URI), her liver was shutting down, she was infested with fleas, and extremely malnourished.

Liz brought Natasha home, along with lots of medications. She had medications for her URI, medications to help her liver repair itself, treated for fleas, and had nose drops. Bunnies don't breathe through their mouths, so it is imperative that you act quickly on anything that may hinder their breathing.

Natasha was treated with Advantage to get rid of the fleas. Not all flea medications are the same, so please check with a bunny savvy veterinarian before using. Ingredients also change, so also check with your veterinarian first.

It took a couple of rounds of medicine to get Natasha healthy, but she was eventually deemed to be in perfect health and ready to be spayed. Seriously, look at that gorgeous hair she has now that she's healthy and well-fed.

Now she enjoys (and demands) her salads and enjoys her morning cuddles on the couch with Liz. She also enjoyed her first Christmas.

If you see a bunny that doesn't belong out in the wild, please don't assume it will be fine. The House Rabbit Society has a great website and Facebook page. There is always someone willing to answer questions or offer advice.

Health and Wellness Tips

The following tips and suggestions are exactly that, tips and suggestions, and should, in no way, replace advice from your veterinarian. Hopefully these tips and suggestions will inspire you to do your own research. Then sit down with your veterinarian and have a list of questions ready to ask him or her.

Spaying/Neutering

Spaying or neutering your bunny is highly recommended. It can help with aggression, litter box training, preventing certain types of cancer and frequent urinary tract infections. Spaying and neutering also prevents unwanted litters, contributing to the overwhelming pet overpopulation problem.

Choking

Choking is common in bunnies. I feel the need to include it in this section because it happened to Suzie. It is often fatal, but it doesn't have to be. Warning signs include bunny pawing at his or her mouth; sneezing; making gurgling sounds; gasping for air; eyes rolling back in his or her head; nose pointing to ceiling, as if trying to breathe; and gums turning blue. If you go to the following web page, you will find demonstrations of the different life-saving techniques. https://www.vgr1.com/choking/ You will even find Suzie's story on this page. These techniques you will learn about are dangerous to perform, but when a bunny is choking, every second counts. It's a good idea to have your veterinarian demonstrate the proper technique, so you will be prepared, if needed. Learning the warning signs and knowing what to do may save your bunny's life.

Healthy Supplies

If your local pet or feed store doesn't have good quality supplies for your bunny, you can purchase them online, like I do. I buy Suzie's hay, pellets, litter, and treats online. There is no reason to be stuck with poor quality bunny supplies. It isn't worth gambling the health of your bunny.

Outdoor Exercise

If you take your bunny outdoors for playtime, please make sure your bunny is safe from predators, running away, and from chemically treated grass. An exercise pen with something covering the top would be ideal.

GI Stasis

GI stasis or stasis is something you hear about a lot in the bunny world. This is when the digestive system slows down or stops. Bacteria builds up and causes the bunny pain, which only causes them to eat less or none at all. Bunny digestive systems need to be constantly moving. A bunny should never go more than 12 hours without eating. It's important to always monitor your bunny's eating and pooping.

Emergency Preparedness Kit

I've seen emergency kits available for purchase. They can be very helpful. Even if you don't purchase an emergency kit, it is a good idea to have the following items on hand at all times. Emergencies seem to always happen at night, on weekends, or on holidays. A good quality recovery food, like Oxbow's Critical Care; dye-free, sugar-free simethicone (infant gas drops); needleless syringes for syringe feeding and watering; ranitidine (Zantac) for possible motility issues; and baby food, stage one, in case your bunny doesn't take to the recovery food. Some veterinarians will give extra Metacam to keep on-hand for pain. You can also purchase emergency kits, if you are unsure of what to include in yours. Seasoned bunny people have kits that look like small pharmacies.

Willow

Most bunnies cannot resist willow. Willow rings, wreaths, and dried, loose leaves are very popular. It's a good idea to at least keep some dried leaves on hand. If you have a bunny who is not eating, you can offer him or her some willow, in an attempt to get your bunny to eat. Leona (right) is checking out her stash.   Photo courtesy of Kim Maring

Master Hope (left), earns his wages by working Quality Control for seasonal Bunny And Friend Wonderful Willow.

Follow Bunny and Friend Wonderful Willow on Facebook.

Photos courtesy of Linda Culbert

The Life of an Easter Bunny is the author's first book. It is currently available on Amazon in paperback and Kindle versions.

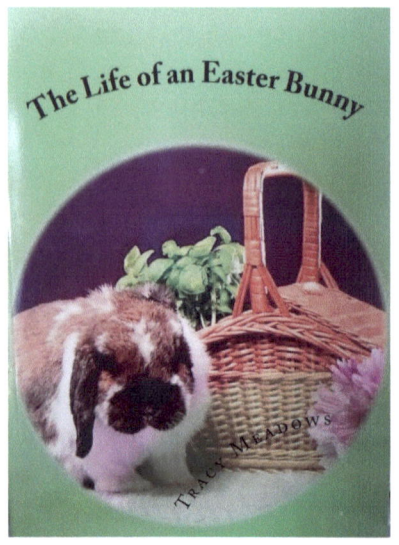

After being put outside alone by her first family, Pounce must learn to survive the outdoors, grumpy old neighbors and meeting other animals before being rescued.

The Life of an Easter Bunny is told from Pounce's point of view and is a must-read for anyone with a bunny in their lives.

"The Do's and Don'ts of rabbit care wrapped in a beautiful story." Dustin Campbell, Bunnyzine

Amazon Reviews

"One notable point: the story is told from Pounce's point of view in the uncommon and entirely refreshing present tense. This immediately allows the reader to be experience each moment and feel the little bunny's emotions as they change from fear upon abandonment to ultimate relief and joy at finding a new home."

"I loved this book! It was both fun and educational. I pick it up and read it all the time. Love the characters too."

"I just finished this book and I can't stop smiling. It is written in the first person - rather first rabbit- which makes is clever, warm and funny. I can't wait to share it with my grandchildren. The author is obviously a bunny owner and sprinkles the story with proper care and maintenance of a pet bunny. A must read for anyone considering giving a home to a rabbit. One caution: reading this will make you want a bunny of your own!"

"I absolutely loved Suzie and her story. This is a book that adults will love to read to children and that children will cherish for years to come. I hope that Tracy continues to write and that we will read more of this adorable one eared bunny."

Special Thanks & Photo Credits

A HUGE thank you to everyone who allowed and trusted me with your precious bunny pictures. Your pictures have added so much to the original idea I had for this book. I thought the book would be about 26 pages. You know, the alphabet has 26 letters. But the more pictures I saw, the bigger the book got, and the book took on a whole new life of its own. Hopefully together, we will be able to educate new bunny people on proper bunny care; make someone thinking about getting think a little harder; and make seasoned bunny people laugh. Thank you so much for your help.

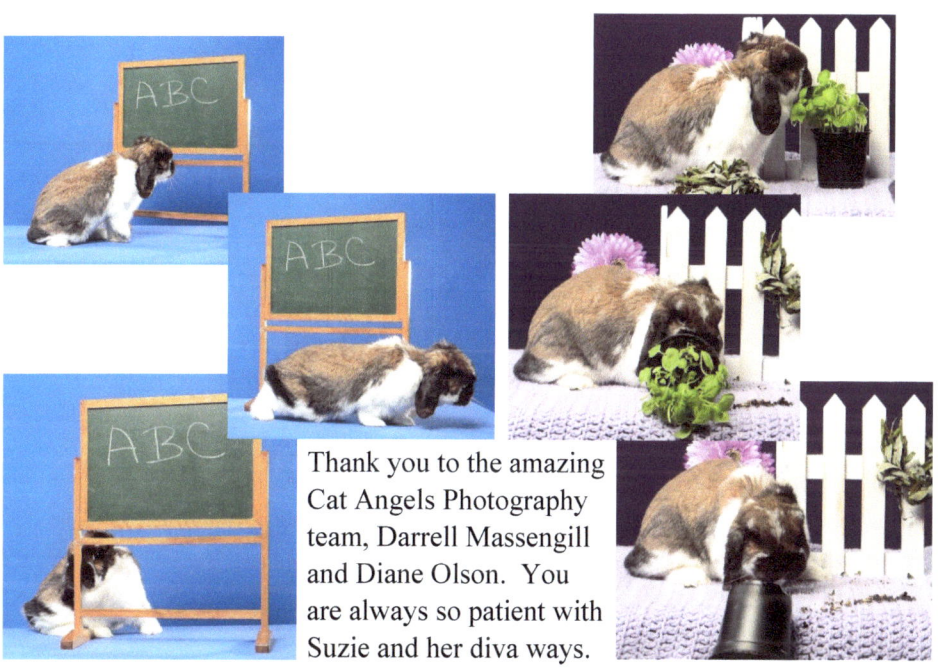

Thank you to the amazing Cat Angels Photography team, Darrell Massengill and Diane Olson. You are always so patient with Suzie and her diva ways.

Photo Credits

Alicia Hodgson	Kate Faust
Amanda Greening	Kathy Pappas
Amie Seal	Katie Cohee
Angie Hutson	Kim Benge
Becky Lemmon	Kim Maring
Brenda Shirley	Kingsley Keiko
Carla Renee	Linda Culbert
Carolina Massie	Lindsey Campbell
Cindy Sanchez	Liz Incardone
Cindy Trivette	Luci Finucan
Colleen Deafenbaugh	Marie Starr
Dawn Haggerty	Marielle Sarkan
Deb Jacobs	Michael ADamowski
Debrah Smith	Michelle Koopman-Miller
Desi Hawkins	Michelle Zeman
Erin Nypaver	Misti Roe
Fern Casey Que	Rebecca Campbell
Gretta Parker	Sandra Lee
Hatka Hrebendova	Sandrine Marquis
Jackie Horalek	Stephanie Gould
Janna Blaydes	Stephanie Pabst
Jenn Eckert	Sue O'Reilly
Jennifer MacLaughlin	Taiya Holden
Joe LaCaille	Tammy Danoff
Johnny Vidster	Tarza Taimur
Julie Barb	Tracey Heaton
Justina Hoflock	Vannissa Kraemer
Kaitlin Rose Scott	Yollie Bloag

The End

Harley

www.ingramcontent.com/pod-product-compliance
Lightning Source LLC
Chambersburg PA
CBHW041641090426
42736CB00034BA/4